What Others Are Saying

Unturned Stones is a remarkable and heartfelt exploration of what it truly means to lead with purpose, empathy, and authenticity. Ranjith Abraham's insights remind us that leadership isn't about knowing all the answers; it's about being courageous enough to ask the right questions, value others' strengths, and create cultures where people feel they belong. This book beautifully aligns with the principles I hold dear—especially the power of creating "learning moments" and leading with a servant's heart. A must-read for leaders seeking to build cultures that inspire and empower teams to thrive.

Garry Ridge
Chairman Emeritus, WD-40 Company & The Culture Coach

Unturned Stones: Exploring a Leadership Dialect for Such a Time as This is a refreshing, personal perspective on leadership shaped by firsthand experience, influenced by other leaders, and firmly steeped in Ranjith's commitment to faith and having purpose in life.

Jordan Berman
CEO, SHIFT Advisory Group

Ranjith's *Unturned Stones: Exploring a Leadership Dialect for Such a Time as This* is a refreshing look at servant leadership. Each page will challenge and inspire the most seasoned leader or newest employee. Leaders are considered stewards of influence, yet we all have areas of influence. Whether we are a parent, employee, or friend, we all shape someone. This book speaks to everyone who desires to shape others for greatness.

Mark English
Lead Pastor, Christian Life Church, Bensalem, PA

In *Unturned Stones*, Ranjith offers leaders a fresh lens to see what truly matters. His words are honest, practical, and deeply inspiring. Each chapter challenges you to look inward, step out with courage, and lead in a way that uplifts people. This is more than a leadership book. It's a call to create impact with humility and purpose.

Rajiv Chelladurai
Author and Leadership Facilitator

Unturned Stones is a masterful exploration of leadership, beginning with the sacred dinner table as the heart of connection, storytelling, and transformation. Through vivid prose and heartfelt wisdom, this book illuminates the power of collaboration, the pursuit of lifelong learning, and the grace found in a culture of forgiveness. It reminds us that the greatest treasures are often found in the bonds of family and the unwavering support of those who journey alongside us. With the infusion of Miles Apart (a band cofounded by Ranjith and his brother) as a soulful backdrop, Unturned Stones is a testament to the beauty of discovery—of ourselves, our loved ones, and the possibilities that emerge for us as leaders when we embrace life's lessons with open hearts. A truly inspiring read!

Rebecca Corbin, Ed.D.
President and CEO of the National Association for Community College Entrepreneurship

Unturned Stones: Exploring a Leadership Dialect for Such a Time as This is an insightful curation of powerful stories and lessons that will help you lead and live more purposefully.

Davin Salvagno
Bestselling author of *Thieves of Purpose* and Cofounder of The Purpose Summit

Every generation of leaders must decide whether they will build on what is familiar or uncover what is true. *Unturned Stones* presses leaders to dig deeper, think more clearly, and speak a leadership language equal to the urgency of our time. Insightful and challenging, this book equips leaders to confront the moment with courage, clarity, and conviction.

Dr. G. Craig Lauterbach
Founder, President, and CEO, CLMIN International

Unturned Stones is a must-read for leaders in every arena. The principles that Ranjith Abraham unfolds serve as both rudder and sail—offering clear direction and forward momentum as leaders navigate familiar and uncharted waters alike. I recommend this book without hesitation.

Steven Rampton
U.S. Navy Commander (Ret.), Author and Entrepreneur

UNTURNED

Exploring a Leadership Dialect
for Such a Time as This.

Stones

RANJITH ABRAHAM

LIFEWORD
publishing

Dedication

This book is dedicated to my father, the late Mr. Abraham Eapen—an ambassador of Christ and a man who embodied what it truly means to lead without a title. In 2026, we mark a decade since his passing, yet his legacy continues to shape countless lives, including my own.

Acknowledgments

To my Creator, the Master Designer. Thank You for choosing me to be a steward.

To my heavenly Father's friend and daughter, Pearly—my wife! I am grateful that your symmetrical thinking paired with my *asymmetrical* thinking creates the balance our family needs.

To my treasures, Zadok and Galilee. I pray both of you will be voices of your generation. Always remember that there are millions of kids in this world who will never know what a chicken nugget is.

To Dad and Mom for inspiring Sujith and me to be purposeful. If not for your support, our dreams would have remained dreams. Dad, wish you were here to read these pages.

To Dadda and Mamma, Pearly's parents, for entrusting me with your daughter. Your investments into our lives are priceless.

To "This is US." You know who you are! Couldn't do life without you guys.

Contents

Foreword

Leadership in today's world is a complex and ever-changing endeavor. It requires not only the courage to confront challenges, but also the wisdom to recognize and act upon opportunities hidden beneath the surface. It's about turning over every stone, uncovering truths, and forging new paths with resilience, integrity, and vision.

Unturned Stones: Exploring a Leadership Dialect for Such a Time as This is more than a guide—it is a reflection of a life lived with purpose, faith, and determination. I have had the privilege of knowing Ranjith Abraham, the author of this extraordinary work, and I can attest that his life journey is a living testament to the principles he shares in these pages.

Ranjith embodies the essence of leadership that this book so profoundly captures. Through his experiences, he has learned the value of resilience in the face of adversity, the power of servant leadership, and the importance of aligning one's actions with a higher purpose. His personal and professional life demonstrates a relentless pursuit of uncovering hidden opportunities and unearthing the potential in people and situations alike.

The phrase "for such a time as this" resonates deeply with the lessons in this book. It reminds us of Esther's story in the Bible, when she stepped into her moment of destiny, risking everything to fulfill a greater calling. Similarly, Ranjith has faced defining moments in his own life—moments where he chose to lead with authenticity, courage, and faith, embodying the very principles he now offers us.

Unturned Stones challenges us to rise to our own moments of purpose. It speaks directly to leaders navigating uncertain times, but still offering timeless truths grounded in faith and wisdom. Through its pages, Ranjith equips us to adapt, innovate, and inspire by turning over the unexamined stones in our lives, uncovering the hidden opportunities beneath them.

This book is not just a leadership manual—it is a deeply personal journey into the heart of what it means to lead with purpose. As you read, I encourage you to reflect on the lessons within, and consider how they might shape your own leadership journey. Whether you are leading in business, community, or personal life, these insights will inspire you to lead boldly, serve selflessly, and leave no stone unturned in the pursuit of meaningful change.

I am honored to introduce this book, knowing that its lessons reflect the life and character of its author. May it challenge and inspire you to step into your moment "for such a time as this," and lead with unwavering conviction and purpose.

Sam Thevanayagam

CEO | Parts Life, Inc. & Deval Lifecycle Support

Introduction

Poor leadership creates villains at the
dinner table.

Whom do you consider a villain? Would you ever imitate that person in real life? Would you invite that person to sit down at your dinner table with you?

Truth be told, most families consider their dinner time sacred—a communal place to gather at the end of the day and converse. It's that special place where we can all let our hair down and share our days together. Kids talk about their teachers and parents talk about what happened in their offices. Those with poor leaders in their workplaces bring their "office" home to the table, often portraying their bosses and coworkers as villains. Perhaps even villains with claws!

There is a chance that my kids, their cousins, and many others whom I love will have an opportunity to work in the corporate realm. This thought has been a strong impetus for me to write these pages—a contribution toward rebuilding the bedrock of leadership. Decades from now, I hope to see that our kids can experience leadership in its truest form—led by shepherds with hearts to serve. As our kids grow up, the investments we make today will help them enjoy better conversations at their dinner tables in the future. No place for villains!

The language of leadership has been spoken as long as mankind has been on earth. Along the way, several dialects have appeared. *Unturned Stones* is a leadership dialect for such a time as this. My intent is to explore a few unturned stones together that will bring forth a revival in the leadership space. Some stones have already been turned, but we will look at them through fresh lenses.

Most unturned stones may cause discomfort, but don't lose heart. Growth begins with discomfort, but it doesn't end there. As we explore the beauty beneath these unturned stones, may God open our eyes to their treasures. Let's begin the journey by exploring Unturned Stone #1: Your Role.

Unturned Stone 1: Your Role

*Executing a vision requires humility
to accept one's limitations. Within the
fibers of this acceptance lie the most
meaningful collaborations.*

In 2009, my brother and I cofounded the band Miles Apart. Although I contribute most of the lyrics and music for the band, I am vocally challenged. When I sit at the piano to write a melody, it is frustrating at times to not be able to hit certain notes. Falsettos seldom help. I would have the entire song playing in my head, even parts to be performed by specific instruments—if only I could sing!

In accepting this limitation, I have developed a superpower to compensate. I envision who can render the vocals for a particular track. Simply put, I use my understanding of whom I can collaborate with to take a song from vision to execution.

So as leaders, what are our roles?

Master Collaborator

The conductor of an orchestra doesn't necessarily know how to play all the instruments, but he or she must possess the uncanny ability to bring an array of musicians together to perform a symphony. That requires a basic understanding of each instrument, how they interact, and what they have to offer. It's the same with people.

It is said that successful leaders are exceptional collaborators. They tend to build teams based on the limitations they have identified within themselves. This begins with letting go of the notion that acknowledging limitations is considered a weakness. In fact, it is the opposite.

LEADEREVEAL (LR) is a leadership video series I host on LinkedIn. It provides leaders with a platform to share the lessons they've learned in their journeys that have had a profound impact on them. Since its inception in October of 2019, more than fifty episodes have been published. I'm going to share some of those lessons in these pages. Here's the first:

> "The real measure of a good leader is someone that can have people around them that have strengths where they are deficient. That's something that I had to learn. At the core of that particular learning was that I had to be comfortable that I am deficient in certain places." (Tremain Davis, LR, episode 45)

Think of one of your favorite products, a movie, or a band. At one point in time, it was probably one person's vision. Without collaboration, that vision would have remained a vision, and never have developed as it has. Collaboration brings us one step closer to reality.

It is key for leaders to surround themselves with people who are smarter than they are. We need to have access to experts in their particular fields. Creating an atmosphere that will foster collaboration among such individuals is the hallmark of a true leader.

> "I am not an expert. Sometimes in this position I have to do so many things. The brochure for principals covers many things—things I didn't even think about…. For me, it is really important to know that there is someone

in the school who is an expert, and I am okay telling you I am not the expert." (Joseph MacClay, principal of Holland Elementary School, LR, episode 61)

Our role as leaders is to create a team of collaborators who will help accomplish a vision that will positively impact lives.

Pilot Igniter

When my family moved into our current home, the previous home-owner was kind enough to walk me through the process of switching on the fireplace. He explained the function of the pilot light, saying, "Although it requires some effort, once the pilot light comes on, it will stay on."

These words have echoed in my mind ever since. As leaders, we need to embrace this truth: There is a pilot light within everyone entrusted to our care, and it's our responsibility to ignite that light. Once it comes on, it will stay on. This gesture will enable those we lead to understand their purpose and the worth of their contributions. The ripple effect will be felt at an organizational level.

Years ago, I remember someone reaching out to me regarding a new job opportunity. He said, "I can see the spark in you. Let's accelerate your career." His offer certainly ignited the pilot light in me.

I am a product of first chances.

Mothership

Let's talk a little about rocket science, shall we? When a spaceship needs to be launched into space, a mothership carries the spaceship to a reasonably high altitude prior to releasing. Once released, the spaceship travels further, accomplishes what is expected, and returns to the ground.

As I became aware of this process, I couldn't help but think about its relevance to leadership. In a way, leaders are like motherships. Our role entails handholding the people entrusted to us until they reach a certain height.

Without motherships, spaceships cannot travel to space. The image of a mothership carrying a spaceship reminds me of safety—and safety is hugely important. Every sheep's unspoken expectation is entrusted to their shepherd, so they are secure.

A friend of mine was hired into a new role and had to learn the ropes—a lot of them. He began confident of being surrounded by help, but to his dismay, in the first year on the job, he was not given the help and guidance he needed. The agenda of each meeting revolved around business updates, and nothing more, making his progress much more difficult.

As leaders, when we hire people we often unplug them from their comfort zone and plug them into uncharted territory. It is true that people make such moves to grow, but it is equally true that they need leaders who can show them the path. The simple act of "checking in" with someone will breathe confidence into their journey. The presence of a mothership is what will help them reach the heights they are meant to attain.

Be willing to witness the caterpillar in the cocoon. Butterflies aren't born. They evolve.

Recently, I had the opportunity to train my son to ride his bike without training wheels. At the onset, he was scared but knew I was right beside him. As much as possible, my son was certain I wouldn't let him fall. He was confident of being in a safe space. By day two, he was on his own, zipping through the community.

Similarly, there are heaps of spaceships yearning to be released. It is time to wake up to the magic of being a mothership.

First Responder

We all know what this title stands for. From firefighters to paramedics, first responders are all lifesavers.

How does this apply to leaders? First responders are trained in putting out a fire or breathing life into someone's situation. These are their key traits. Good leaders need the ability to be the *first one* to say, "I don't know."

Recently, I watched a video in which a drummer and his sound engineer were reviewing the microphones that made his drums sound the way they did. At some point, the sound engineer mentioned a brand of microphones, and the drummer said, "Never heard of them." He didn't know!

One of the greatest drummers ever was acknowledging that he didn't know which microphones made his drum kit sound so superb! I paused and reflected on this. Leaders are often hard on themselves for not knowing all the minute details, but we need to constantly remind ourselves to not be trapped into such a delusion. We're not supposed to know everything.

Garry Ridge, the former CEO and Chairman Emeritus of WD-40 Company, believes in "tribe culture." In his book, *Tribe Culture: How It Shaped WD-40 Company*, Garry says, "One of the turning points in my own life and career was the day I got comfortable with the three most powerful words I ever learned: 'I don't know.'"[1]

"As leaders, our greatest blessing is the people we lead.
We must gratefully tap into the knowledge they possess.

---

1. Garry Ridge, *Tribe Culture: How It Shaped WD-40 Company* (S.l.: Garry Ridge, 2020).

Leaders aren't expected to know it all. Such a mindset is a self-imposed constraint.

"I don't have to be the smartest guy *in* the room, but I do have to get the smartest idea *out* of the room. That is leadership." (Pastor Mark English, LR, episode 23)

Encore

- Leaders need to play the roles of master collaborator, pilot igniter, mothership, and first responder.

- Our role is to create a team of collaborators who will help accomplish a vision that will positively impact lives.

- Leaders need to embrace the truth that there exists a pilot light within everyone entrusted to their care. It's their responsibility to ignite that light.

- A mothership carrying a spaceship is focused on its safety, which is every sheep's unspoken expectation from their shepherd.

- Leaders aren't expected to know it all. Such a mindset is a self-imposed constraint.

Unturned Stone 2: Culture

*Establish a culture so deeply rooted in
values focused on your employees that
people on the outside consider your
organization a cult. In fact, they want to
experience your cult.*

Now that we are past the first unturned stone of knowing our roles as leaders, it will be exciting to embrace one of its fruits: a people-centric culture.

I was a newbie at one of my jobs. A few former colleagues belonged to a different team within the same business unit. As I was settling in, the first thing that stuck out was the stark contrast between the organizational culture and the culture within my team. Specifically, the organization promoted the "work from home" concept on a need basis, so every employee needed access to a laptop.

While my colleagues on the other team enjoyed the luxury of having a laptop and working from home once a week, my team was expected to be at the office five days a week. It must be noted that working from home would have had no negative impact on productivity. In short, the leaders on my team created a culture that was by no means advantageous to any of the team members. As a result, the morale of the team was quickly eroding.

Old school of thought? Lack of trust? I will leave it to your imagination.

At a later point, I was able to initiate conversations with senior management which led to our team being provided with laptops and the provision of working from home on a need basis.

An employee-focused culture is the cure to most issues that cause decay to the organizational fabric. The actual culture in a workplace goes far beyond a well-worded culture statement or fancy theory. Many times, the culture statement is not reality, but the desired state.

No matter how much an organization boasts of its culture, the actual leader determines the version of the culture that each employee experiences. Leaders must become cultural ambassadors. Yet another role!

As leaders, we *are* the culture.

Let's explore a few pillars that will strongly contribute toward creating a people-centric culture.

Culture of Investments

My dad and mom were serious investors—not the kind the word *investor* usually evokes, but investors nevertheless. They invested in people and things that built people. Back in the day when money was tight, they sacrificially invested so my brother and I could have access to musical instruments. I can confidently say that their act of love has borne fruit.

In today's corporate realm, seldom do we come across organizations that genuinely invest in their people. Even though their people are their greatest asset, "growth without investments" is the preferred mantra. Someone once told me, "Budgets don't budge!" Really?

In his book *Finding Purpose at Work*, my friend Davin Salvagno asks: "Who are we helping others become?"[2] The person we help others become is directly proportional to the investments we are willing to make.

It is important to wake up to the truth that investments cannot be "one size fits all." Every employee's career aspirations are unique. Some will be interested in becoming leaders, while others enjoy being individual contributors in roles of increasing responsibility. Prior to investing, it is essential for leaders to gauge who an employee wants to become. This means being intentional about spending time with people to understand them better—beyond the surface.

Just like custom-tailored clothes, custom-tailored investments aren't cheap. Imagine the impact such investments will have on employees. Think of every good trait expected in employees. Those traits are the byproducts of the intentional investments that are made.

Sam Thevanayagam, my mentor and CEO of Parts Life Inc., knows exactly what a custom-tailored investment is. Through a novel initiative titled "Help U Buy," Parts Life offers a forgivable loan to employees to help them buy homes.

In Sam's words: "We want every single person who works for us to be part of the American Dream. When you own your first home, that sets you up for everything else. It gives you stability." The impact of such an investment on employees, their families, and communities is beyond belief.

Culture of Forgiveness

There is a notion that it is impossible to weave forgiveness into the corporate realm. Let's just say that's a myth. Forgiveness is a form of kindness. It is the simple understanding that we are all human and all humans make mistakes.

---

2. Davin Salvagno, *Finding Purpose at Work* (Cork: BookBaby, 2020).

Basic psychology tells me that employees cannot survive in an unforgiving culture, let alone thrive. Their minds will be conditioned to approach every task with questions that begin with "What if…"

According to Garry Ridge, mentioned in the last chapter, there are no "mistakes," only learning moments. In Garry's words from his book, *Tribe Culture: How It Shaped WD-40 Company*, learning moments are "positive or negative outcomes from any situation that needs to be openly and freely shared to benefit all."[3]

A culture of forgiveness calls for learning together with no finger pointing. It entails creating checks and balances to avoid repetitive mistakes.

Even geniuses slip!

I have been fortunate to watch some of my favorite bands perform live. Every now and then, these legends inadvertently hit what I call a bum note. Unless you are a musician, chances are you may not even recognize a bum note. The truth is even if a bunch of musically sound attendees hear a bum note, they aren't throwing a fit. They continue to enjoy the show, acknowledging the fact that the legends on stage are fully human, prone to errors. I have never heard anyone say, "I'd like a refund!"

What happens after someone hits a bum note is special. Instead of unleashing fury, at least some of the band members will walk over to the one who made the mistake, laugh, and move on. Camaraderie in its truest form takes center stage.

The word *authenticity* has gained a lot of traction lately. We need to remind ourselves that people will not bring their authentic selves into a culture that reeks of unforgiveness.

---

3. Garry Ridge, *Tribe Culture: How It Shaped WD-40 Company* (S.l.: Garry Ridge, 2020).

Culture of Recognition

Cognition, a powerful word derived from *recognition*, means perception. Let's look at recognition as a sort of "re-perception."

Today, a lot of employees perceive themselves as a cog in the machine. A grain of sand. A number. This unhealthy perception is mainly due to the fact that their contributions are not recognized. There isn't any worth attributed to the work they perform. The impact of such a negative perception is manifold; hence the absolute need for a culture of recognition.

How does an employee like to be recognized? Note that I used "an employee" in the question. We need to see this from their perspective, recognizing that each person is individual and unique. Similar to different love languages (words of affirmation, quality time, etc.), there ought to be multiple "recognition languages." One size does *not* fit all.

To recognize is to empower.

Personal

A few months back when my wife asked me what I would like for my fortieth birthday, I said, "Please don't get me anything. Let's go on a trip to London with the kids."

Having read and heard so much about Virgin Atlantic's customer service, we wanted to experience it for ourselves. Instead of flying out of Philadelphia, we braved the traffic, drove to New York, and flew out of JFK on Virgin. Best decision ever!

On the way back, while in the air, I mentioned to a cabin crew member that we had been to London to celebrate my fortieth birthday. Later, without my knowledge, she approached my wife to confirm my name.

A few minutes later, the crew member came by with a package. It contained a handwritten birthday wish, a Virgin Atlantic coffee mug, and a few other goodies. I couldn't have asked for a better ending to the trip. For the first time, I wasn't thinking of tiredness as I disembarked. As a family, we were leaving an experience—one that we would love to repeat. Love at first flight!

Here was an employee representing a brand, recognizing a customer's reason for joy, and tailoring an experience. Let's swap the roles, shall we? How magical would it be if leaders took the time to create such meaningful recognition experiences for their people? There's no better way to win loyal employees.

I remember my wife receiving a response to an email she had written to the then-CEO of the company she worked for. The company had more than 100,000 employees. Likely, it is one of the most valuable emails in her inbox! If electronic communication can be so powerful, consider how much more impactful a physical note can be.

There is something special about handwritten notes, and they're even better if they are notes of recognition. Like all magical experiences, creating them takes time. Such efforts carve indelible memories in the minds of employees and make them feel cared for.

Another form of personalized recognition is to offer paid time off. There are people in our workforce who would appreciate this gesture more than anything else—especially in a corporate ecosystem like the one in North America where the number of paid leaves are much less than those found in other parts of the world. Such recognition will go a long way. Words will not suffice to describe the joy this will bring to an employee who would like to attend their child's piano recital or simply have some "me time."

Let's go back a decade. My dad was ailing and since it was the end of the year, I didn't have too many paid leaves left in my account. I wanted to go to India and spend time with Dad. Some of the senior executives at the organization recognized my need and offered a solution.

They asked me to put in some work over the weekend to complete a few critical tasks and then take the time I required to visit Dad. Generosity through recognition!

Public

Either at an employee gathering or via digital communication, employees that are publicly recognized for their contributions gain a strong sense of belonging. This helps them understand how their work is impacting the big picture. As a result, they will begin to experience a sense of purpose at work.

Monetary

A monetary recognition is certainly of some worth too, especially if an employee's contribution has resulted in thickening the bottom line. Still, even a monetary recognition can be customized. A gift card to an employee's favorite store or restaurant will double the impact. Such acts will exponentially increase the genuineness of the recognition you are trying to convey.

Let's explore a unique flavor of recognition.

- Why is the attrition rate so high?
- Why is employee engagement at a record low?
- Why are we struggling to attract the right talent?
- Why do employees seem miles apart from the organizational purpose?

The above questions are usually echoed in boardrooms. Solutions are based on what leaders have seen and heard from their tower of power. While this is not entirely the wrong course of action, most leaders seem to miss the boat, which you discover only when speaking with their employees on the ground.

"Part of the unlearning process is being humble about the fact that I don't know everything. I am happy to learn. By doing that, you actually win the trust of your team. You win the respect of your team…. Sometimes the folks that are very close to the problem know and are in a better position to articulate the problem to you."
(Dr. Kiran Krishnan, LR, episode 14)

Employees on the frontlines see and hear what leaders don't. When their peers exit the organization, it is likely that they have heard the real story in contrast to what was shared at the exit interview. Employees may also know of potential reasons why external candidates aren't considering your organization a green pasture.

Have you ever considered the degree of recognition offered to employees when their feedback is requested and considered? Taking action based on the input received will help convince employees that leaders are intentional about building a people-centric culture, a culture where employees are recognized for what they really know, beyond their jobs.

> # Proposing a solution without appropriately analyzing the issues at hand is like stitching a suit when the real need is for an undergarment.

Appropriate analysis is speaking with those on the frontlines. Those individuals are our assets. So leaders, let's engage and recognize real problems.

Culture Coaching

Corporations need to take into consideration the presence of multiple cultures in the global ecosystem. Although organizations take pride in their corporate culture, the individual cultures of those who form the workforce must not be ignored.

I have had the privilege of working with organizations wherein the workforce was based in India and North America—essentially a culmination of two complex cultures that are vastly different. Since I had worked in India for a few years prior to immigrating to the United States, I was aware of the cultural nuances. At least, most of them. It made the interactions with my counterparts pleasant and contributed toward the productivity of the team.

Oftentimes, corporations will appoint individuals to lead teams that are global, but offer them minimal to no support in being culturally competent. The outcome of this recipe will be a half-baked cake!

Respecting one's culture is vital. It is the hallmark of genuine leaders to invest time in understanding the cultural elements of their team members, clients, stakeholders, and so on. When leaders are culturally competent, it portrays a spirit of collaboration and humility.

Deshika Rodrigo sheds light on the power of culture coaching on LR. In her words:

> "You take them through a series of coaching where you actually discuss things like how do people communicate, what is appropriate, what is not. What are the little subtleties." (Deshika Rodrigo, LR, episode 41)

Leaders need to ensure their people are capable of flexing their cultural muscles appropriately, so the role of a culture coach is vital. Offering the support of a culture coach is, in fact, an investment toward an individual's success. Without intentional help, maneuvering the cultural labyrinth can become a nightmare.

Encore

- No matter how much an organization boasts of its culture, every employee's leader determines the version of the culture that they experience.

- "Who we help others become" is directly proportional to the investments we are willing to make.

- A culture of forgiveness calls for learning together with no finger pointing. It entails creating checks and balances to avoid repetitive mistakes.

- Similar to the different love languages—such as words of affirmation, quality time, etc.—there ought to be multiple recognition languages.

- Employees on the frontlines see and hear what leaders don't.

- Leaders need to ensure their people are capable of flexing their cultural muscles appropriately.

Unturned Stone 3: How Are You?

*When our focus is to change someone's
world for the better, success is inevitable.
Such transformation is inexplicable.*

Years ago, I was on a flight to Toronto. As we entered Canadian airspace, I heard the captain say, "If you are seated on the left side of the aircraft, look out the window in a minute. You will see the falls." My wife and I had been to Niagara Falls before and its beauty was etched in my memory. Still, I had the curiosity of a child to get a glimpse of them from up in the air.

With my face almost glued to the window from 30,000 feet, they looked like a speck. There was no way I could sense their foaming, roaring splendor. Upon landing, one thing was certain: Niagara Falls was teaching me a lesson—the need to get close to people.

Let's ask ourselves if the view we have of our people is up close and clear—or from 30,000 feet. If it is the latter, chances are we will never know who our people really are. If we do not know their values and their circumstances, how can we lead them?

We commonly ask the question: "How are you?" The habit of asking that has been around for a long time. However, what I don't know is this: When did this very powerful question become closed-ended. When we walk down the street or come to a register at a store, we hear different versions of that query.

How are you?

How's it going?

How's everything?

We typically respond without any true circumspection. We say we're good or great, even stellar, but we don't stop and consider how we are truly doing. When did we begin to answer it so quickly?

I dodge this question as much as possible, and have learned to reserve it for truly intentional moments. Remember that when we ask someone how they are, we are making a commitment to listen to them. We really want to know how they are doing.

> # Asking someone how they are is like knocking on a door, expecting someone to open it, and then welcome us in.

In today's corporate world, this question has lost its place. Even if the question is asked, the expected responses are scripted. The most powerful question we have to help us understand how someone is doing has been desensitized. This should not be.

As leaders, we ought to often ask this question of our people *with intention*. With the utmost genuineness.

The "How Are You?" Hour

In most cases, one-on-one meetings are all about work. Deadlines. Expectations. Conversely, the "how are you?" hour meeting is designed with solely that three-word question in mind. It's the only question the leader is required to ask.

It is key to help our people understand the intention behind this hour. They need to know that glib answers like good, great, or even stellar aren't going to cut it. This hour is their opportunity to let down their guard and speak candidly. This includes sharing information about their families, health, and so on, to whatever extent comfortable. It's the leader's opportunity to listen and get to know the one who is working for them on levels that are not all about the workplace.

Like everything else, the first "how are you?" hour might not last an hour! Building genuine relationship takes time, but eventually, this practice will enable leaders to develop a holistic perspective of their people and help them lead better.

As leaders, let's be careful not to:

- Prescribe solutions to any issues presented unless an employee specifically seeks guidance. Just listen. Don't endeavor to fix.

- Judge! Our people must know that this hour is a judgment free zone.

The Pause

As humans, we are wired to seek *the pause* during a dialogue so we can start talking. The question is, "How long must the pause be before we grab the mic?" While it is not fair to define this by a number, leaders must gauge the temperature in the room.

There is a good chance that when executed with intention, the "how are you?" hour will encourage employees to pour their hearts out. In short, vent. While sharing sensitive information, instances of a *long pause* are to be expected. At such moments, it is key to *hold ourselves back from saying anything.* The silence helps the other person understand that we are listening. We are processing. We are not rushing.

Employees might share about an ailing parent, issues with kids, frustrations at work, and so on. Tears will be common. Keep a box of tissues handy! I have noticed that the more sensitive topics are, the longer the pauses. Wait as long as possible, and follow your reply with: "Would you like to share more?" Continue to listen, and if time runs out, be flexible, or promise to schedule a follow-up session at the earliest convenience for you both.

How often should leaders schedule an hour like this? Let's allow our people to decide, shall we? (I can hear some of you thinking: *My job description needs to be revised!*)

As with everything else, set expectations. Employees do realize that as shepherds, our plates are full to overflowing. Allowing them to decide the frequency of your meetings enables them to reach us when they need us the most. When a child gets hurt, we don't wait to administer first aid, do we?

Being available to intentionally ask how your employees are and listening to them are two of the most important responsibilities of a leader.

How can adopting this special hour as a practice shape us as leaders?

Better Listeners

Time and time again, we have heard about the power of listening. The act of genuinely asking someone how they are offers opportunities to actively listen. And it must be genuine. We know the difference between someone perfunctorily going through the motions, doing the right thing, and one who is truly engaged and listening to us. Needless to say, cellphones don't belong in spaces where such meaningful conversations take place.

Intentional

As much as it is important to be great listeners, this practice needs to be complemented with timely follow-ups. For example, if an employee shares about the upcoming wedding of a child, it is appropriate to remember the date, possibly send a card, and ask a timely question or two about the wedding. Now, we are getting beyond the surface. Believe it or not, when our questions are intentional, we are showcasing togetherness. Be it celebrating a milestone or standing with our people during hard times, being part of a team is strengthening.

> "Now I go throughout my day as a leader trying to be tiny. Trying to be small. Trying to embrace every little tiny moment, living ten seconds at a time, and in that ten seconds, being fully present in every conversation with everybody I come across, and really trying to just love people in that moment." (Mike Thompson, LR, episode 21)

Empathetic

When we understand who our people really are, it helps us to grow in empathy. Many consider *empathy* a buzzword. In point of fact, it is a mindset. It is the ability to relate to another's situation. Simply put, it makes us human.

Let's explore some obvious connectivity here. In the previous chapter, we discussed the culture of recognition and how seeking feedback from employees is a form of recognition. The "how are you?" hour can also be considered a platform for employees to share their thoughts on what needs to change and how they can contribute.

As leaders, we need to come to grips with the truth that success means something different to each person. The most common school of thought around success is rooted deeply in its monetary aspects. For some, money might be the only measurable standard for success. However, in today's world, there are scores of employees on the other end of the spectrum, and they define success very differently. To some, success is seeing an idea become reality, while others find success in developing meaningful relationships.

Irrespective of how employees define success, it is our responsibility as leaders to help each of them be successful. So the time we spend getting to know them grants us the opportunity to understand what success means to each individual.

Ceiling Microphones

A few weeks ago in church, I noticed two microphones hung from the ceiling. It intrigued me and reminded me of an earlier conversation. These microphones capture the voice of the audience. When a familiar hymn is sung, the congregation participates by singing along. There are times when this is such a beautiful experience that the band will mellow down so the congregation can be heard more fully.

Leaders are often in the forefront making decisions. We get caught in a maze in which we are often deafened by the extreme decibels of corporate noise. If we do not intentionally check on them, we will not hear our people. Their feedback is invaluable. In your journey as a shepherd, are you enjoying the participation of your sheep? If not for literal ceiling microphones, what mechanisms have you installed to hear your people? Take a moment and make a list and evaluate their usage and efficiency.

Encore

- Remember that when we ask someone how they are, we are making a commitment to listen to them. We really want to know how they are doing.

- Being available to intentionally ask how your employees are and listen to them are two of the most important responsibilities of a leader.

- Believe it or not, when our questions are intentional, we are showcasing togetherness.

- The time we spend getting to know each employee grants us the opportunity to understand what success means to each individual.

Unturned Stone 4: Communication

Like everything else, communication is easier when the skies are blue. As clouds roll in, communication with our people experiences a bit of turbulence. The truth we often forget is that employees are normal human beings. We all go through the cycles of life. Let's explore a form of communication that will help us in hard times without compromising its dignity.

T-R-A-C-E Communication

Transparent

I love how the word *parent* is nestled within *transparent.* As parents, my wife and I expect our kids to be transparent with us; we also expect their teachers and physicians to be transparent with us. Since transparency is a foundational pillar to meaningful connections, it is challenging for me to think of these relationships without it.

It is vital for leaders to be transparent with their people about the impact their subpar performance has on the bigger picture—on the organizational vision. The power of such transparent communication must not be undermined. Leaders must never assume that their people will figure it out. Wouldn't we talk to our kids if their grades were dipping?

Transparency is the beat for the march of solidarity.

Let's change our lens. Think of workplace scenarios wherein we have thought: *If only they were transparent.* Often, when an employee's performance is on a downward spiral or there is a drastic change in attitude, leaders are left to assume what the problem might be. Let us tie this back to the "how are you?" hour. As relationships gain depth from the multiple meetings they have had with you, there will be an elevated level of trust and transparency. They will begin to confide in you with greater confidence and less anxiety. They will believe that being transparent is the best choice.

> "Fear of being liked or being disliked because of asking the hard questions has the tendency to push leaders into a space where they operate in a vacuum."
> (Jason Harris, LR, episode 8)

It is important to remember that transparent communication will only be effective if, as leaders, we choose to be pleasantly transparent when our people deliver stellar performances and kindly transparent when things are not going as well. This builds the culture of recognition on every level, as we discussed earlier.

Crabbing: A Different Approach

Have you ever noticed aircrafts occasionally descending for a landing with their noses pointed on an angle, not parallel to the runway? I have. Intrigued, I learned that this is an aircraft landing technique known as crabbing. When the wind is not favorable, pilots adopt this landing approach. Although it may seem anomalous to the onlookers, pilots know what they're doing. There is a reason they are expected to be good at math!

Based on business needs, leaders need to adopt their own crabbing techniques. Our people might be of the opinion that the aircraft is about to crash. Employees will begin to envision the business crumbling like the walls of Jericho. While we calculate a particular approach, let us not assume that our employees will understand the nuances of our decisions. Only the shepherd knows the destination. Sheep simply follow. Being transparent with our teams on *what* is being done and *why* is critical to achieving our mission.

Respectful

If we were to create a recipe for communication, respect would be a key ingredient. Relationships are torn apart when there is a lack of respect in communication.

Ever been in situations in which all your past accolades were trampled upon and you were cursed and about to be thrown into the lion's den? I have!

Communication without respect accelerates the erosion of trust.

Our communication—with everyone at all times—must be respectful, especially during times of crisis. Truth be told, when our people are going through hardship and their performance is being negatively impacted, they do not need one more burden to rob them of their dignity. They would rather have a shoulder to lean on—a leader with whom they can be transparent, knowing they will be treated with respect. A leader who is a refuge and not a threat.

When we struggle to communicate respectfully, it is important to ask ourselves if we have any underlying biases, intentional or unintentional. What is the remedy if we test positive for bias?

Pause! Before we utter words that cannot be taken back, in humility, we need to let the employee know that the conversation will be continued later when we are in a better frame of mind. We must also ask employees to be transparent when leaders are not communicating respectfully. Leaders, be ready to receive such feedback gracefully.

> "It is hard for someone to voice how they are feeling when those feelings may not be well-received, particularly when they see you as their leader. As a leader, that is an opportunity we have to embrace, even if we don't agree." (Deirdre Van Nest, LR, episode 31)

Authentic

Authenticity is paramount in the realm of communication. Unfortunately, the words *phony, fake,* and *inauthentic* are commonly used to describe the communication style of many leaders. We have all been around people who say and do things only to impress those around them. They work hard to create a persona that is far from real, and it is worlds apart from their authentic selves. Too bad, it all sticks out like chicken pox! If they only knew!

In his book, *The Trust Trifecta*, my friend Jordan Berman says, "Leaders are often challenged with communicating authentically because it's difficult to get them to be vulnerable when they believe they must be perceived by others in a certain way."[4] Let us look at an example to understand what authentic communication really is.

---

4. Jordan Berman, *The Trust Trifecta: A Leader's Guide to Hitting the Trust Jackpot* (Toronto, Ontario: Iguana Books, 2020).

When missed deadlines become a norm rather than an exception for an employee, here are two potential versions of communication from a leader:

- Everything is going to be okay. Let's keep moving.
- We do have a challenge before us. I am here to help in any way possible. Let us work together to accomplish the organizational goals.

I will leave it to your imagination as to which response is authentic!

Another setting in which leaders sugarcoat their message while talking with an employee and complain and call down fire on that same person when they're not around is far too common. A leader cannot act in pretense, but must build real relationship through honesty or they build walls instead. By design, if leaders struggle to communicate transparently and with respect, authentic communication will remain an illusion. The bottom line is that inauthentic communication stifles an employee's individual growth and jeopardizes organizational success.

Authentic communication will always imbibe the values of an organization and serve as a microcosm of the larger organization. One can say that when communication is layered with transparency and respect, it also becomes authentic and rings true.

Clear

The Eagles is a band that requires no introduction. Think of the guitar solos from songs like "Hotel California" or "Get Over It." Even better, consider taking a few minutes to listen to those classics. They are crafted intentionally and articulated so clearly through their guitars that they are recognized immediately and remembered forever. This is the approach we must adopt while communicating: Communicate clearly. I can guarantee that those attending an Eagles concert will be able to hum a tune by the time they leave the show. Simple melodies are powerful and grip us internally. In most songs, melodies and choruses are repeated. Repetition creates clarity, so the information remains in our brains longer and is readily accessed. This takeaway is golden.

As leaders, we need to find ourselves repeating pertinent information. After offering an explanation, we need to ask a follow-up question like: "Does that answer bring clarity?" This habit is vital to our communications. Depending on the gravity of the question, you can create even more clarity by detailing the question afterward in an email. This will eliminate any room for misinterpretation.

Empathetic

Having been in the pharmaceutical labeling domain for more than a decade, I am aware of the laborious nature of the job. A simple typographical error could mean a delay to a critical product launch. Although technology has advanced, there is still need for human intervention, which results in occasional errors.

In LR, Navin Mathew quotes his uncle as saying: "Principles may never take you up, but they will never let you down." (Navin Mathew, LR, episode 30)

In my leadership journey, I've put out many fires. Every so often, those fires were the result of human error. Since I was well-versed in having made those errors in the past, communicating with empathy was my only choice. I utilized these opportunities to share personal stories to help my people understand that they were not alone in the game. I reminded them that stars never cease to shine. (This is science!) Through respectful probing, I tried to gauge the potential roadblocks they were dealing with—personal or professional. Then, I considered how my empathetic communication could be translated into empathetic acts.

> "What you see initially may not be the truth. Assume positive intent…. Be good to everybody. Everybody is having a tough day." (Chester Elton, LR, episode 50)

Communicating with empathy does not mean sweeping things under the rug or condoning mistakes. Together with our people, we need to acknowledge that there are challenges and explore more effective ways of working on tasks that will mitigate risks. When our communication is transparent, respectful, authentic, and clear, chances are it will culminate in communication that is also empathetic.

Encore

- It is important to remember that transparent communication will only be effective if, as leaders, we choose to be pleasantly transparent when our people deliver stellar performances.

- When we struggle to communicate respectfully, it is paramount to ask ourselves if there are any underlying biases—intentional or unintentional.

- Authentic communication will always imbibe the values of an organization and such communication from leaders will serve as a microcosm of the larger organization.

- Repetition creates clarity; therefore, the information remains longer in our brains and is more readily accessed.

- Communicating with empathy does not mean sweeping things under the rug or condoning mistakes.

Unturned Stone 5: Purpose

*Purpose is what wakes us up. It keeps us
up at night. It makes us smile. It lets us
be authentic. Purpose presents the best
version of ourselves to the world.*

Purpose is the reason behind existence—the "why" beneath actions and outcomes.

This is the reason for which we exist.

My mom and dad were missionaries. Straight out of college, they identified their purpose and decided to live it out—fully. For the sake of purpose, they moved from one state to another in India. One home to another. One apartment to another. I can confidently say that purpose was their guiding star.

My parents always had just enough, and at times, a little less. A life with no frills. Yet they were rich! Purpose compensated for all the things they lacked. Purpose meant something to them. Perhaps it meant everything.

Impactful world changers like Mahatma Gandhi, Nelson Mandela, and Mother Teresa are fine examples of people who lived purpose-ful lives. They did not pursue a specific career that aligned with their purpose; instead, their entire lives revolved around purpose. Purpose became the nucleus.

> "Whether you are leading a business, a non-profit, or a church, at the end of the day if you have a purpose that you really believe in—that you align with, and if you are leading yourself well toward that purpose and the values of your organization, then it becomes so much easier. It just becomes natural to be able to lead others with passion." (Robin John, LR, episode 44)

It is important for leaders to know their purpose—the real reason for their existence. The question is, how do we identify our purpose? As leaders, this is critical.

Self-Awareness

We often ask ourselves questions like: "Who am I?" or "What are my unique abilities?" My kids would likely answer this question, "My ability is to fire up my dad like a V8 turbo engine without as little effort as possible!" The answers to these questions could be instant or not. If need be, we must give ourselves time to reflect, so we can arrive at the best answers and better understand our purpose. When each of us can identify our purpose and direct it toward the greater good, the outcome will be magical—like a symphony.

Learn to Listen

Self-awareness can be complemented by listening. I hope each of you has a meaningful group of friends. I call it the inner circle. Those who belong to our inner circle will take notice of what excites us and vocalize it. These signs, from those we love, are signs of what we are capable of offering the world—our purpose.

Be Focused on Others

Although purpose is *within* us, seldom is it *about* us. So if we are self-aware and listening to others and we wish to advance, it is time to reevaluate. Just like thorns pointing outward, actions that are birthed from our purpose must be focused outward rather than inward—on others rather than us.

Imagine being a wedding photographer. It is time to capture a moment with the bridal party. Twenty people! What do we do? We pick up our wide-angle lens because we need a broader perspective. We need to ensure that everyone is in the frame. Let's look at purpose through a wide-angle lens.

It is critical for shepherds to understand the life purpose of each of their sheep. Has anyone at work ever asked you about the purpose for your life? I can imagine the likely answer.

As leaders, let's make a commitment to tear down this wall and talk to our people about purpose—and not just organizational purpose, but *their* life's purpose. Through self-awareness, listening, and focusing on others, purpose can be better understood—theirs as well as our own.

Let us once more tie this to the "how are you?" hour. As those hours progress, there is a good chance employees will reveal more of themselves. Leaders will be able to gauge what really brings out the passion in their people—beyond work.

In fact, as new people are entrusted into our care and we get to know them, consider asking this question: "What is your purpose?" The understanding we gain will create a holistic perspective of our people and positively impact the way we lead.

Think of the phrase "subject matter experts." This refers to anyone who specializes in a particular content area. As leaders, we must be in a position to replace the words "subject matter" with the names of our people: "John expert" and "Jane expert" and so on. This will enable us as leaders to lead the whole person and not just a part of the person.

Understanding the life purpose of each employee also presents another priceless advantage. *It makes us aware of their innate gifts*—those that are not necessarily listed on a resume. This will come in handy when certain positions that require a specific skillset need to be filled.

Needless to say, purpose is a two-way street. When employees understand that their individual purpose is valued, it becomes easier for them to come on board with the organizational purpose.

In his book *Finding Purpose at Work*, Davin Salvagno says, "As an individual we can have many purposes, some more important than others, and those are the ones we often do not get paid for."[5]

When leaders value the purposes of their people that they don't get paid for, those employees will value their purpose at work that they do get paid for.

Still contemplating the value of purpose? Please travel with me back in time.

John was a senior executive at an organization. Many of his peers considered him an effective communicator. Based on results from an employee survey, John was asked to deliver a speech on purpose at a company-wide event.

Valuing the opportunity before him to impact at least one person, John curated the content for his speech and had it validated by the event organizers. John was set. After delivering the speech, John received a standing ovation, and in the weeks following, many of John's peers witnessed the ripple effect of his speech.

One day, John received a meeting invitation from someone named Joe with whom he was not familiar, but he accepted the invitation anyway. After researching, John understood that Joe was fairly new to the organization. On the day and at the time of the meeting, a young man showed up

---

5. Davin Salvagno, *Finding Purpose at Work* (Cork: BookBaby, 2020).

in his office and introduced himself as Joe. Joe thanked John for his time and mentioned how impactful his speech was.

John sensed there was more to Joe's visit and asked, "So Joe, how are you doing?" Joe began sharing his story by saying his father was ailing. Music was Joe's livelihood—his life's purpose. To cover his father's treatment expenses, he needed supplemental income. Then he said, "I like my job, but don't love it." The box of tissues came in handy, as John could relate to Joe's story.

John thanked Joe for his candor and promised to support him every way possible. A few minutes later, to satisfy his curiosity, John looked up Joe on a social media platform. What he discovered blew his mind: Joe was an epic entertainer. A one-man show. John, aware of an employee recognition event coming up, approached the event organizers and shared Joe's music with them immediately and without a second thought. They were surprised that such talent existed in their organization and unanimously decided to feature Joe at the event.

John was creating a platform for Joe to live out his purpose at work.

The next day, John walked over to Joe and shared this news. Joe's eyes welled up. He hugged John and thanked him.

On the day of the event, Joe's performance mesmerized the crowd. In fact, they asked for more. When Joe got off the stage, John ran to him, hugged him, and told him how proud he was of him.

A week after the event, John received another meeting invitation from Joe. John gladly accepted and excitedly looked forward to their conversation. When Joe showed up, there was a sense of grief. Even before John could say anything, Joe got misty. He told John that his dad had passed away the night of the event. The next few moments were marked by a long hug and heaps of tissues. John was genuinely empathetic, as he had experienced a similar loss not too long ago.

After a while, John asked Joe if he would continue his job as its purpose was now fulfilled. Joe took a few seconds and said, "I have grown to love my job. Someday, I want to help someone the way you helped me. I am going to stay." Needless to say, John was thrilled.

The next day, John received an invitation from senior leadership requesting him to meet with them. Not certain of the agenda, John accepted the invitation and the following day met with some senior executives in the organization. They presented John with an opportunity to move into a new role—one that would focus on leadership development within the organization. This would also entail building a new team.

John was speechless and gratefully accepted the offer. Knowing that the people required to accomplish this mission had to have their heart in the game, he thought of Joe right away. Without even consulting Joe, John walked over to Joe's manager and presented the pitch. Fortunately, there was no resistance.

Actions birthed from purpose will define our legacy. It is what we will be remembered for.

When John shared this news with Joe, hugs and tissues joined hands again. In the next two weeks, John and Joe began to work together. Today, I have been told that Joe is involved in highly purposeful work, impacting lives.

Leaders need to embrace the truth that not everyone on their team will consider their jobs to be purposeful. Some jobs can be mundane—a sequence of tasks. As leaders, we still need to help our people understand how their contributions impact the organization. Also, it is key to become aware of any purposeful initiatives that employees are involved in outside of work, and showcase our support toward them.

Encore

- It is critical for leaders to know their purpose. It's the real reason for their existence.

- When leaders value the purposes of their people that they *don't* get paid for, those employees will value their purpose at work that they *do* get paid for.

- As leaders, let us make our people aware that through self-awareness, listening, and focusing on others, purpose can be better understood.

Unturned Stone 6: Credentials

Stones and slings can do what swords cannot.

Many of us are familiar with the story of David and Goliath in the Bible. It's one of my favorites, and my kids love it too.

Here is the short version: A very long time ago in Israel, the Philistines waged war against the Israelites. David was an Israelite shepherd boy and Goliath was a Philistine giant, the enemy. When Israelites with better stature than David feared the giant, David decided to face the giant head-on. Just as he already cared for and defended his sheep, David realized his purpose was also to save his people.

Saul, the king of Israel, tried to help David look the part by lending him his armor, but with the king's heavy armor, David could barely move. He was not comfortable. He left it behind and picked up five smooth stones and a sling instead. Goliath taunted David because he looked so weak and small, but David struck Goliath down with the first stone!

Recently, I was introduced to a new word: *credentialism*. It describes a tendency to place excessive weight on formal education when evaluating people. Reliance on credentials does not take into consideration a large scope of other factors that each employee brings with them.

As a newbie at one of my previous jobs, I was getting to know my team members. One day at lunch, a team member said, "Ranjith, you're fortunate to have a college degree. I have already been told that there is no more growth possible for me, and in my life today, college is not an option." I was stumped. The job was far from requiring a college degree. I could not imagine the morale of employees like this one who had become a victim of meaningless protocols.

The corporate world loves the hype around degrees, even when they are not necessary. The story of David and Goliath clearly illustrates this truth. It wasn't the king with the armor who slew the giant, but the shepherd boy with his five stones.

Leaders in the corporate world need to come together to change the status quo. There is a lot of talk about being inclusive, but the growth of many is stifled merely because they lack an unnecessary degree! That's a far cry from being inclusive.

What are we naturally good at doing?

If the story of David and Goliath were to be made into a movie, I am certain the most anticipated scenes would be their confrontation and then the moment when David walks over to King Saul with Goliath's head—the ultimate sign of victory. Still, I would like to steer our attention to another magical moment in the story that has a thought-provoking take-away for leaders.

It came much earlier in the storyline—before the battle. It was in the preparation.

As mentioned before, David decided not to wear the king's armor. There's no hint in the story that the king was angry about that, and he could have acted very differently. King Saul could have insisted on David wearing armor, however unwieldy it was. He also could have exercised his authority and held David back from fighting the giant in the first place! A loss meant the king and his subjects would become slaves to the Philistines. The stakes were high! There is also no record of the king even being aware of what weapon David was planning to use to fight Goliath.

Instead, the king trusted David to slay Goliath and was humble enough to allow him to use weapons that he could wield. A sling and stones were comfortable for David. They were natural to him. King Saul did not micromanage David; he let him use his natural bent to solve the big problem of Goliath.

> "As the leader, we are supposed to have the strength and the wisdom and the knowledge to make the right decision and do the right thing without the filter of personal consequence or gain. Without pumping the brakes and the consternation of making that decision." (Mike Vacanti, LR, episode 49)

Consider all that a leader learns from the many one-on-one meetings they have with their employees. The purpose of those intentional hours together is to help people understand their life's purpose. Conversely, leaders become better equipped to lead when they are aware of and in tune with their people's natural abilities.

Let's revisit Joe's story from the previous chapter. When John fueled Joe's natural gifting (music), it changed the trajectory of his life.

The corporate world seems to be caught up in the top-down approach. Leaders love to dress their people. Responsibilities are assigned without considering someone's natural abilities. If only we would take the time to tap into our people's innate gifts! The sky is the limit.

Another story will help solidify this truth. Recently, I came across a new band. At one of their shows, the drummer's in-ear monitors malfunctioned and he managed to let the stage crew know of this fiasco. The drum technician came to the rescue with two basic tools: his hands and a drumstick. He could hear the entire band, so he began to tap the drummer's foot with his hand and the drumstick. This ingenious solution enabled the drummer to play almost flawlessly, so the band was able to perform the entire set.

The drum technician was playing the role of David against his Goliath—the malfunction in the in-ear monitors. Drum technicians set up equipment and handle the technical aspects of a show. It's a real full-time job! The in-ear monitors are used by musicians during live performances to allow them to hear themselves and their fellow band members, so they're vital.

For all the right reasons, the technician could have stopped the show until the glitch was rectified. Instead, his presence of mind allowed him to tap into his own natural skills. He trusted the ability of the drummer to adapt, and they worked together. What a show!

On another note, people sometimes accept a position to get their foot in the door, even though they are not convinced that a job aligns with their natural giftings. Often, with some on-the-job training they will be off to the races. This makes it all the more important for shepherds to put in the effort to know the natural abilities of their sheep. When positions that align with an employee's natural skills open up, leaders need to advocate on their behalf. A leader's words should be validated and must offset the lack of formal credentials.

Think of the impact this approach could have. Understanding an employee's natural gifting and helping them move into an appropriate position are elements found in both a "culture of investments" and a "culture of recognition."

Encore

- Stifling the growth of an individual because they lack an unnecessary degree is a far cry from being inclusive.

- As leaders, we will be better equipped when we become aware of our people's natural abilities.

- Understanding an employee's natural gifting and helping them move into an appropriate position are elements found in both a culture of investments and a culture of recognition.

Unturned Stone 7: Art of ComplEmenting

To work in harmony is to complement
one another.

When I published my first article on LinkedIn, a kind reader pointed out a typographical error I had made. I had used *compliment* instead of *complement*. To be clear, the word *complement* describes something that completes or enhances something else—like how a side dish can bring balance to a main course. It should not be confused with the word *compliment*, which refers to offering praise or expressing appreciation, such as thanking someone for a job well done. They are very different concepts, and over time, my love for the word *complement* has deepened. I have begun to consider it an art.

If there is a critical art form that leaders need to master, it is the art of *complementing* other leaders and helping their people *complement* one another.

I am a musician, so I may be biased, but there is no better medium to fall in love with the art of complementing than music! Since we spoke about The Eagles earlier, let's continue the journey.

The Eagles typically had four guitar players on stage, including the bass guitar. To watch four guitarists gracefully perform a complex musical passage is quite a treat. There are some interesting perspectives involved in that approach. Someone once told me that "four guitar players meant a *lot* of sound." While this is true, there is so much more to it. Let's explore a concept in music called *harmony.*

A great example of harmony can be found in the song "Hotel California." Whether you are a fan of rock or not, chances are you have heard this anthem at least once. The song is structured so uniquely that the moment someone hears the first few notes, they recognize the song. They recognize the band. No need for a music app!

As a musician, I can vouch for the complexity involved in accommodating four guitar players in a band. There is no value in such an arrangement if all the guitarists perform the exact same parts. There is no value in overplaying either. It will just be a lot of noise. Each player has to identify a part that will *complement* the parts played by the other guitar players. It takes an incredible amount of effort to achieve this feat. However, when the parts are played together, it is epic. It is magic. It is *harmony!*

Let's recreate a concert stage with the departments of our organizations. Think of the people on our teams. Most often, there is a power struggle. Everyone likes to be in the limelight. Everyone wants to be the loudest—all the time. There's no limit to the number of times people pose questions such as, "Who is better?" or "Who is at fault?" or "Who is more creative?"

A competitive spirit is healthy, but a spirit of division is not. Leaders must encourage their people to complement each other while they are competing. Now that's a feat.

Having been in the pharmaceutical industry for many years, I have been exposed to the complex process of bringing a new drug to the market. There are so many stakeholders involved, and at times it can get messy. At one of my jobs, my team was involved in designing the artwork that went on the packaging components (bottles, cartons, and so on). The graphics my team created had to complement the packaging components, and the packaging components needed to complement the manufactured product. There was no putting it on the market without all three pieces coming together as seamlessly as possible.

While departments needed to complement each other's work, they also had to complement each other's timelines. My team was expected to deliver our design as the product was being manufactured. It didn't make sense to have a product sitting around without its design and corresponding packaging components ready to go.

The recent pandemic caused by the coronavirus saw the art of complementing in action. Industry leaders came together to help the world. It caught the attention of many when two pharmaceutical giants, Johnson & Johnson and Merck, joined hands to help slay the Goliath that was challenging all the modern scientific advancements. In spite of not being able to bring its own vaccine to the market, Merck dedicated some of its facilities to manufacture the vaccine created by Johnson & Johnson. Wow! Rivalry was traded for camaraderie.

There's no doubt that these are great examples of collaboration. I am of the firm belief that the art of complementing forms the bedrock of collaboration.

If your search for a square fails, seek two triangles instead.

This quote was inspired by a game that my kids love to play called Marble Run. One day, we were in desperate need for a square to complete a formation. Luck showed up in the shape of two triangles. My kids were thrilled. I was, too! I still remember them screaming, "Dad, two triangles make a square."

As leaders, when faced with Herculean challenges, we often tend to look for one resource—one person who can subdue the giant. When the search fails, our frustration is obvious. What if we looked for two triangles instead? What if we searched for two individuals who excelled at complementing one another's skills and timelines?

Imagine one guitar player having to perform *all* the intricate, differently tuned guitar parts in "Hotel California" all by himself or herself. The outcome is highly questionable.

Without a doubt, the art of complementing will help leaders and their teams get many steps closer to accomplishing the organizational purpose they want to achieve.

Encore

- If there is a critical art form leaders need to master, it is the art of complementing—complementing other leaders and, in turn, helping their people complement one another.

- A competitive spirit is healthy, but a spirit of division is not. Leaders must encourage their people to complement while competing.

- The art of complementing forms the bedrock of collaboration.

Unturned Stone 8: Expectations

*Irrespective of circumstances, all
employees are greeted every day by an
usher with arms wide open and long
bear hugs. Expectation!*

have had the privilege of working with some amazing individuals from India. These are some of the most hard-working people I have ever known. Some of them had to use three modes of transportation just to get to work. You read that right. Three! Bus, train, and a cab (or at times, an auto rickshaw). Their commute was approximately two and a half hours—one way. Air conditioning was not part of this picture. Once their tired frames got past the entry door, their employer's expectations kicked in immediately.

Even before the pandemic, I was a proponent of working remotely for at least a few days every week. This demanded a paradigm shift. A difficult one.

I found myself asking the following questions time and time again:

- How can I expect these employees to be productive?

- How can they be focused?

- How is work-life integration possible for these individuals?

I guess the pandemic had an answer! When employees had to work from home, their attitude was that of gratitude. In addition to keeping themselves and their loved ones safe, they were now able to spend quality time with them, enjoy meals together, and even tuck their kids into bed. Expectations at work may have been slightly elevated, but employees met them graciously.

I remember someone telling me, "Ranjith, I can't believe this is possible."

Circle of Thirds

The circle of thirds is an important concept in music theory. I will refrain from delving into the specifics, but suffice it to say that it's a handy method for organizing and remembering chords.

Let's apply it to our lives by taking a deep dive into one day—twenty-four hours. A third of this is eight hours, and it is the amount of time an individual spends at work—at least. Another third should be spent resting and another in wearing the many hats we each wear: spouse, parent, child, sibling, student, friend, and so on.

Let's focus on the third spent at work. How an individual feels at the end of their eight hours at work will determine the quality of their time at home with family and friends and the many activities involved with all of that. Undoubtedly, this will go on to impact the quality of their rest too—the final third.

When expectations at work are unreasonable, the negative impact is felt at home. Let's go deeper. When an individual returns home disgruntled and is expected to open their "black box" (a corporate reference to their laptop) again, it impacts relationships. It robs the individual of the opportunities they might have to wear other beautiful hats, such as that of a spouse or parent.

Once relationships are negatively impacted, the quality of rest takes a hit.

When leaders identify employees who are missing the mark, TRACE communication needs to kick in. There is a good chance that there are issues on the home front that are negatively impacting their rest. It could be an ailing parent or a child. If need be, for a period of time, expectations need to be altered. Responsibilities have to be revisited. This is being kind. This is being intentional. This is being empathetic. This is leadership in action!

Sleep deprivation is a form of torture. How can productivity be a byproduct of torture?

I remember a time when an employee had to take his child for regular appointments every Friday afternoon. When he described the situation to me, I immediately recognized that he shouldn't be tapping into his paid time off for this. Instead, we worked out a new schedule wherein he could finish all his work by Friday afternoon and take the time off he needed; expectations were met both ways. In fact, an employee who is catering to an ailing child or parent deserves a vacation more than anyone else. It is unfair to have such an individual tap into their paid time off so they can be at appointments.

While leaders have expectations of their people, it is important to know that people have expectations of their leaders as well. Let us tie this back to the many ideas we have considered together thus far.

- *Leaders are expected to be master collaborators, pilot igniters, motherships, and first responders.*

- *Leaders are expected to cultivate cultures of investments, forgiveness, and recognition.*

- *Leaders are expected to regularly and intentionally ask the question: "How are you?"*

- *Leaders are expected to communicate transparently, respectfully, authentically, clearly, and empathetically.*

- *Leaders are expected to know their purpose and help their employees identify their purpose as well.*

- *Leaders are expected to boycott credentialism.*

- *Leaders are expected to master the art of complementing.*

Let us explore another expectation people have of their leaders.

Accessibility

Leaders often claim that "their door is wide open." The irony is that usually, there is no one on the other side of the door.

Imagine a herd of sheep trying to reach their destination without a shepherd. Lack of communication leads to a lack of safety. There is no sense of belonging. The fact is that people need *all* of those things—communication, safety, and a sense of belonging.

> "When I took on this role, many people said to me, 'You are not going to be able to engage with students as much as a president.' …It just seemed so wrong to suggest that somehow you play into the stereotype of a president who is perhaps inaccessible, out of touch, and not representative of their stakeholders." (Dr. Ajay Nair, President of Arcadia University, LR, episode 43)

Leaders need to be intentional about making themselves accessible to their people. Based on the current climate, it could be in person or virtual, but people need to believe that they are not in a sheep-without-a-shepherd ecosystem. Leaders need to realize that they cannot fulfill their roles without being accessible. Accessible leaders are essential for healthy cultures.

Encore

- When expectations at work are unreasonable, its negative impact is felt at home.

- While leaders have expectations of their people, it is important to know that people have expectations of their leaders as well.

- Leaders need to realize that they cannot fulfill their roles without being accessible.

Unturned Stone 9: Shepherd's Wallet

*As a leader, the fine print in your job
description reads 'willingness to open
your wallet.'*

All work and no play makes me a dull boy! At one of my jobs, the concept of team outings did not exist. Around Christmas, I initiated a team lunch. I wasn't sure what to expect, but the team responded warmly and assumed that our leader would find a way to reimburse the lunch expenses.

Everyone enjoyed a fine Italian meal. Leaning back on the couch, I thought to myself, *This is a good start.* Minutes later, when the check was brought to the table, the unthinkable happened. I heard the leader say, "That will be $30 each." The look on some of my colleagues' faces is still vivid in my memory. Needless to say, it was the one and only team outing.

The truth is that the leader did not even bother to check if there was a provision for a team lunch. Additionally, the leader was more than able to foot the bill for six people.

Erosion of trust? Respect? A lot happened in those two hours. I walked away from that lunch learning what not to do as a leader.

I am aware this is a sensitive topic, but it needs to be discussed. Bringing coffee for an employee or taking the team out to lunch doesn't have to be confined to Hallmark movies. Leaders ought to open their wallets and express their generosity.

Time to swap lenses!

A friend of mine was traveling to India to visit family. Since he had direct reports who lived in a different part of India, it made sense for him to seize the opportunity and meet these individuals in person. His leader completely dismissed the idea.

A $100 round-trip ticket to enjoy time with his team wasn't going to put a hole in my friend's wallet, so he paid for it. Let's just say his experience was priceless. He couldn't stop talking about the elevated level of engagement and camaraderie that resulted from his trip. It was the result of the act of opening his wallet.

As leaders, we should not always depend on corporate wallets. We must tap into the power of our *own* wallets and embrace opportunities to celebrate our people. Generous leaders exude warmth. Think of the ripple effect. We might be able to influence the thinking of at least one person. It is one little way of changing the world around us.

One more lens swap! This story has had a profound impact on me.

Amanda was a leader who hosted a very special team activity every year during Christmas. She would ensure the entire team participated. The activity was to spend a whole day at an adult day care. Amanda would spend a considerable amount of her own money to buy lunch and gifts for the folks at the day care.

For the longest time, her team assumed the expenses were covered by the organization. When they realized this wasn't true, it was a shocker. This act of opening her wallet solidified all the values that Amanda portrayed at work. She was living out her values.

Many of Amanda's team members had their own teams. They were so inspired by their leader's generosity that they all devised their own special team activities, tapping into the power of their own wallets. Ripple effect at its best.

Such acts have an effect on the heart. Remember how we discussed leading the whole person and not just a part? I don't believe it can get better than this. As the Bible says, "What you say flows from what is in your heart" (Luke 6:45, NLT).

As leaders, we need to have our hearts in the game. We tend to ignore the role of the heart in how we shepherd our people. The purpose we strive for, cultures we cultivate, and the way we communicate depends on the health of our hearts. It depends on what our hearts are filled with.

Robin John, CEO and founder of Eventide Investments, sheds light on an academy for women that he and his wife, Jaunita, helped establish in India:

> "These are young women that come from backgrounds where they don't have the same opportunities, so we want to empower them to believe in themselves. These are young women that really care to transform their communities, and the whole country and the world." (Robin John, LR, episode 44)

Examples such as this solidify a mantra I believe in:

Thrive by helping others thrive.

Encore

- Leaders ought to open their wallets and express generosity.

- As leaders, we should not always depend on corporate wallets. We must tap into the power of our own wallets and embrace opportunities to celebrate our people.

- The purpose we strive for, cultures we cultivate, and the way we communicate depends on the health of our hearts. It depends on what is in our hearts.

Unturned Stone 10: Shepherd's Staff

*Design a shepherd's staff for the safety
of your staff.*

A shepherd's staff is a long and sturdy stick with a hook at one end. It is used by a shepherd to manage and sometimes catch sheep. However, its versatility does not end there. The staff may be used to defend sheep against attack by predators. When maneuvering rough terrain, the staff acts as an aid to balance. Shepherds also use the staff to part thick undergrowth when searching for lost sheep or potential predators.

Matt is a leader who has a real shepherd's staff in his office. He has quite a few tags attached to the staff. Some of them read as follows:

- Watch each other's back

- Empathy

- Kindness

- No cursing

- No judgments

- Forgiveness

Just when I thought this was epic, I was told that every new hire is introduced to this shepherd's staff. Matt takes the time to explain how much he and the organization value a safe workplace. Then he takes it up a notch by asking the new hire if any additional tags need to be added to the staff.

Wow! Occasionally, if Matt hears of any employee issues related to emotional safety, he takes the time to have a one-on-one "how are you?" hour with the employee, during which time he reintroduces the shepherd's staff. It is an act of reassuring the employee that safety is his top priority.

When maneuvering rough terrain, the shepherd's staff acts as an aid to balance.

Let's dive a little deeper into this idea. As leaders, we encounter rough terrain. We also find ourselves scrambling for aid to get through it. A shepherd's staff is what will help us maintain balance.

I had the privilege of enjoying Matt's storytelling skills. His organization was gearing toward a critical product launch—one that had the power to change the trajectory of the company. A lot of logistical arrangements were made to celebrate this milestone.

Hours prior to the launch, Matt received an unexpected call. It was from Suzanne, the newly appointed head of compliance. For the first few seconds all Matt could hear was Suzanne's labored breathing. Not certain if the issue was related to Suzanne's family or work, Matt said, "Suzanne, I am here. Talk to me."

In the next few minutes Suzanne explained that an oversight from her team would force them to hold off the launch. Suzanne was not definitive about how much time it would take to iron out the wrinkle.

Matt felt as if someone was clobbering him. Being the man he is, he kept his cool and requested that Suzanne would call for an emergency board meeting. In the next hour, Matt was in the board room. So was his shepherd's staff. Suzanne and the rest of the board members trickled in.

Suzanne's success story as an immigrant was familiar within the organization. However, the board was still in the throes of adopting a mindset of cultural diversity, and this contributed to Suzanne's anxiety.

Even before Suzanne could present the issue, Matt addressed the board. He held up the shepherd's staff and said, "Irrespective of what we are about to hear, each of us will honor every word written on the shepherd's staff. We will not operate in any other way."

Imagine the impact these words had on Suzanne. She presented the issue to the board, honestly expecting a strong backlash. Below are a few responses she received:

- *Suzanne, I can't imagine how this must be crushing you. We are in this together.*
- *Suzanne, we've got you. What can we do to help?*
- *Suzanne, this is certainly a big blow. Yet this is an opportunity for us to come together and acknowledge we are human too. Humans make mistakes.*

Matt was shedding invisible tears of joy as he witnessed the shepherd's staff come alive. He thanked the board and promised that he would work with Suzanne to obtain the required clearance and have a revised launch date at the earliest possible time.

Needless to say, Suzanne was deeply grateful to Matt for watching her back. "I would have it no other way," Matt assured her later. Matt and Suzanne worked together with their teams and were able to launch the product later that week. As forecasted, the product changed the trajectory of the organization—in more ways than one.

Every now and then we come across questions that leave an interviewer stumped. Recently, I heard this exchange.

Interviewer: *Do you have any questions for me?*

Candidate: *How does the organization ensure an emotionally safe workplace?*

Interviewer: *Let me get back to you.*

Hmm. When in the market for a new home or a car, one of the first items we research is safety.

- *Is it in a good neighborhood? What is the traffic like on this street?*

- *What safety features are available in that car? Does it have automatic braking?*

We are all familiar with these questions, so it should be no surprise when a potential candidate asks about the safety features of the organization where they are interviewing. It is a shame when we don't have answers.

> "In workplace, we ignore the fact that we are all human. We are all going to feel the pinch. Again, if we just make an assumption that the person is in one particular way and you *don't* create the environment where you are prepared to hear the hard things and…open up the space to talk about it and make them feel comfortable being able to tell their truth, then the truth won't come out." (Heather Younger, LR, episode 7)

Envision a scenario where Suzanne was not forthcoming with Matt. If fear of retribution held her from sharing the truth, what would have been the outcome?

As leaders, it is paramount to create an emotionally-safe workplace. Have you designed a shepherd's staff? If so, what does it look like? If not, it is never too late. I encourage you to take the time to do so—and remember to ask your sheep what they would like to see on the staff.

Encore

- When maneuvering rough terrain, the shepherd's staff acts as an aid to balance.

- It should be no surprise when a potential candidate asks about the safety features of the organization for which they are interviewing.

- Remember to ask your sheep what they would like to see on the shepherd's staff.

Till We Meet Again

enjoy watching my son board the school bus. In his younger days, he would see it coming down the road and look out the window at the yellow bus and ask, "When can I get on that bus?"

Recently, my son and the school bus got me thinking. Imagine a child who asked the following questions before boarding the bus.

- *Is the pressure on all the tires ideal?*
- *Have the tires been rotated?*
- *How much gas is in the tank?*
- *Is the state inspection complete?*

I can confidently say that these questions have never come out of the mouths of any kids I know. They simply trust the bus driver and the school authorities to ensure the basics are done correctly. Now, if a *red* bus showed up tomorrow morning, perhaps there would be a question or two! I'm pretty sure there would be.

When employees join an organization, they are entrusting themselves into the care of its leaders in the same way—especially to their immediate leader. Employees should not have to be detectives in finding out if the basic elements of leadership, such as empathy, humility, integrity, and so on are a part of their new ecosystem. Like kids boarding a school bus, employees should be able to simply trust that the organization is built on a strong foundation—just like the wise man who built his house upon the Rock.

If leadership is a bus, _______ must be one of its wheels.

A friend and I coauthored a few articles together, and came up with this statement. To fill in the blank, we came up with "wheels" like integrity and humility. Take a few minutes to reflect and identify at least four wheels that will form the foundation of *your* leadership. Everything else must be built on this foundation.

We have explored a lot of territory while reading this book, and I hope these words have encouraged you. Perhaps you have only travelled a short distance in your leadership journey so far. (Maybe, you haven't even begun yet! That's okay.) The point is that you have a lot of food for thought—a lot of "wheels" to consider for building your bus.

Please consider these "unturned stones" and join hands with me in speaking a leadership dialect for such a time as this—for the sake of our kids, our families, and all those in this world who might someday be a part of the corporate realm. Then choose a dialect that reflects your values, just as I have.

Each of us must be honest about who we are. Everything is connected. Just as those wheels turn so the bus can move, the engine gives it power. That speaks of your inner core. Your belief system. What matters most to you.

Who am I?

A sinner saved by grace.

"For God so loved the world that He gave His only begotten Son, that whoever believes in Him should not perish but have everlasting life" (John 3:16).

I love Jesus. Yes, I do! I believe in Him and want to treat others with love and respect because it honors and pleases Him to do so. I want to truly love others as I have been loved.

Expecting someone to be quiet about their faith is like inviting a leopard to dinner without its spots.

About the Author

Born to missionary parents in India, Ranjith immigrated to the United States in 2010, and considers it a blessing to be a husband and a father. He lives by the mantra: "Thrive by helping others thrive." In that vein, he desires to transform the corporate world into a space that exudes a sense of belonging by pointing leaders back to the basics. As a qualified engineer, Ranjith has worked for fifteen years in the pharmaceutical regulatory domain in a variety of leadership roles and has a passion for people. He volunteers his time serving in the church band and being a trustee of a nonprofit organization that focuses on providing education to kids in particular impoverished communities. His online devotional "The Second Shout" and his band "Miles Apart" are humble attempts at exercising stewardship.

Ranjith can be contacted at **unturnedstones@ranjithabraham. com** or by visiting **ranjithabraham.com**.